Jane Clarke

Select Portions of Psalms and Hymns Set to Music

with the thorough basses carefully arranged for the organ or pianoforte

Jane Clarke

Select Portions of Psalms and Hymns Set to Music
with the thorough basses carefully arranged for the organ or pianoforte

ISBN/EAN: 9783337103866

Printed in Europe, USA, Canada, Australia, Japan

Cover: Foto ©Lupo / pixelio.de

More available books at **www.hansebooks.com**

of
PSALMS and HYMNS
SET TO MUSIC

with the Thorough Basses carefully arranged

for the

ORGAN, or PIANO FORTE,

as Sung at

OXFORD, WELBECK, & PORTLAND CHAPELS

St Mary Le-Bone.

The Second Edition Corrected & Improved.

Printed & Sold by R.t Birchall N.o 133 New Bond Street
and by the Editor N.o 110 High Street, St Mary Le-Bone

Price Five Shillings.

To
The Revd. Sir Richard Kaye Bart. L.L.D.
Dean of Lincoln;
and
Minister of St. Mary Le Bone;
THIS COLLECTION
of
SACRED MUSIC
Is humbly dedicated
By his most Obedient
and grateful humble Servant
Jane Clarke.

INDEX

Psalm		Page
1	Albury	1
4	St Mary	2
8	St Davids	3
9	Manchester	4
13	Brunswick	5
15	Oxford	6
16	Boston	7
19	Messiah	8
22	Weston Favel	9
23		10
25	Bath	11
27	St Matthew	12
33	Doncaster	13
34	Abingdon	14
36		15
37	Cary's	16
40		17
57		18
67	Invocation	19
71		20
73		21
77	Whitton	22
84	Wheatfield	23
91	from Artaxerxes	24
93	Hotham	25
95	Westminster	26
97		27
100	Savoy	28
103		29
104	Hanover	30
105	St Georges	32
106	New Court	33
107	Mecklenburgh	34
108	New Jerusalem	35
111	St Dunstons	36
113	All Saints	37
115	Bedford	38
118	Foundling	39
119	St Andrews	40
121	St Anns	41
125	St James's	42
130	Mount Ephraim	43
133	Wiltshire	44
135	St James's Chapel	45
136	Portsmouth	46
138	from Judas M^c	47
139		48
145	Bedford Chapel	49
146	Cambridge	50
147	Lincoln	51
148		52
149	Adeste Fidelis	53
150	Tavistock	54

INDEX

Hymns	Page
1 Morning	57
2 Evening	58
3 New Year	59
4 Epiphany	60
5 January 30th	61
6 Lent	62
7 Good Friday	63
8 Easter	64
9 Ascension	65
10 Whitsunday	66
11 Trinity	67
12 May 29th	68
13 The Kings Accession	69
14 November 5th	70
15 Advent	71
16 Christmas	72
17 Sacrament	73
18 Charity	74
19 Charity	75
20 Fast Day	76
21 Thanksgiving Day	77
22 Funeral	78

Albury Ps. 1 C.M. Scott

2
But makes the perfect Law of God
  His Business and delight,
Devoutly reads therein by day,
  And meditates by Night!

3
Like some fair Tree, which fed by Streams,
  With timely Fruit does bend,
He still shall flourish, and success,
  All his designs attend

4
For God approves the just Man's Ways,
  To Happiness they tend;
But Sinners, and the Paths they tread,
  Shall both in Ruin end!

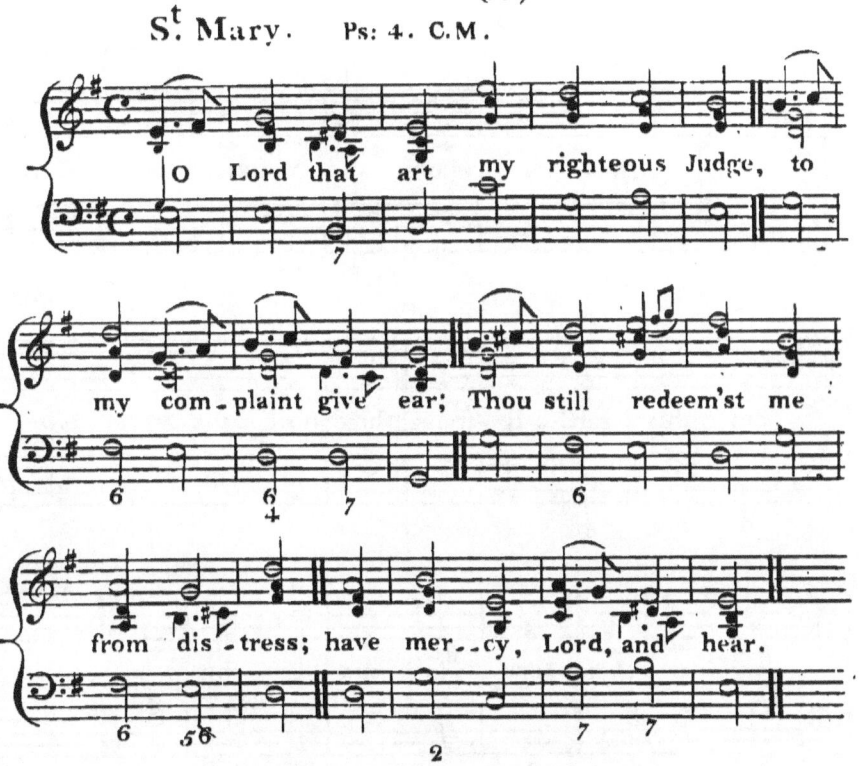

S.t Mary. Ps: 4. C.M.

O Lord that art my righteous Judge, to my com-plaint give ear; Thou still redeem'st me from dis-tress; have mer--cy, Lord, and hear.

2

    Consider, that the righteous Man
      Is Gods peculiar choice;
    And when to him I make my Pray'r,
      He always hears my Voice.

3

    While worldly minds impatient grow
      More prosp'rous Times to see,
    Still let the glories of thy Face,
      Shine brightly, Lord, on me.

4

    Then down in Peace I'll lay my Head,
      And take my needful rest;
    No other Guard, O Lord I crave,
      Of thy defence possest.

2
When Heav'n, Thy beauteous Work on high,
　Employs my wond'ring Sight,
The Moon, that nightly rules the Sky,
　With Stars of feebler Light;

3
What's Man, I say, that, Lord, thou lov'st
　To keep Him in Thy Mind?
Or what his Offspring, that Thou prov'st
　To them so wond'rous kind?

4
O Thou, to whom all Creatures bow,
　Within this earthly Frame,
Thro' all the World, how great art Thou,
　How glorious is Thy Name!

Manchester   Ps. 9 C.M.   Wainright

To celebrate thy Praise, O Lord, I will my Heart prepare To all the listening World thy works Thy wond'rous works declare.

2
The Thought of them shall to my Soul
   Exalted Pleasure bring;
Whilst to Thy Name, O Thou Most High,
   Triumphant Praise I Sing.

3
All those, who have His goodness proved,
   Will in His Truth confide;
Whose Mercy ne'er forsook the Man
   That on His Help relied.

4
Sing Praises therefore, to the Lord
   From Sion His Abode;
Proclaim His Deeds till all the World
   Confess no other God.

Ps: 13 C.M.

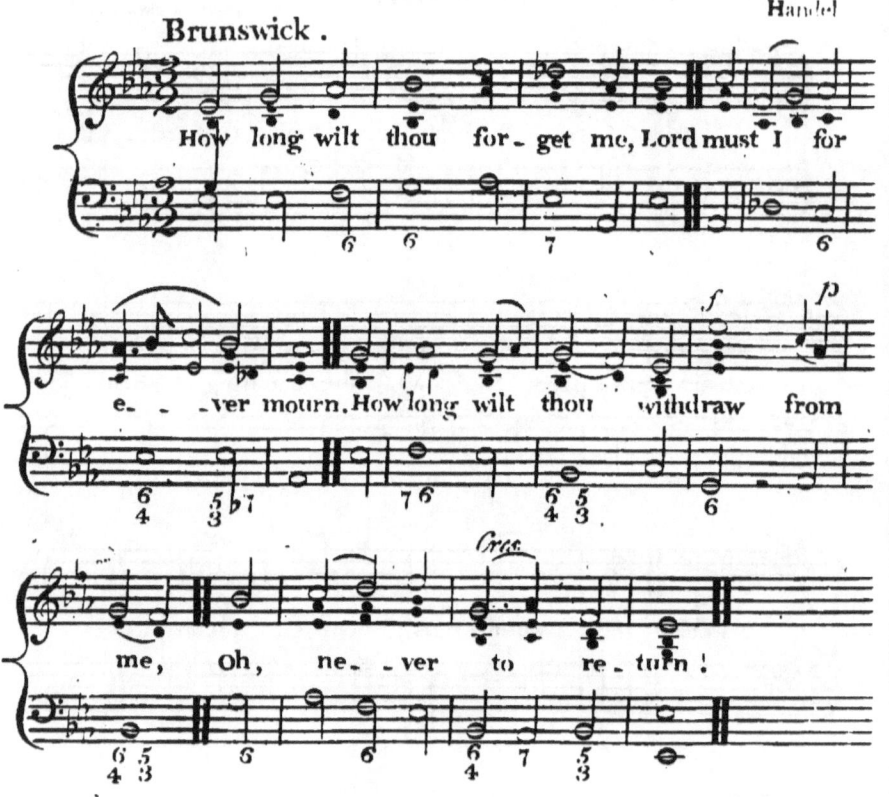

Brunswick. — Handel

How long wilt thou for-get me, Lord must I for e——ver mourn. How long wilt thou withdraw from me, Oh, ne——ver to re-turn!

2
How long shall anxious Thoughts my Soul,
  And Grief my Heart oppress?
How long my Enemies insult,
  And I have no Redress?

3
Since I have always placed my Trust,
  Beneath Thy Mercy's Wing;
Thy saving Health will come; and then,
  My Heart with Joy shall spring:

4
Then shall my Song, with Praise inspired,
  To Thee, my God, ascend,
Who to Thy Servant in Distress,
  Such Bounty didst extend!

2
'Tis he whose every thought and deed,
  By rules of Virtue moves;
Whose gen'rous tongue disdains to speak,
  The thing his heart disproves.

3
Who never did a slander forge,
  His Neighbours fame to wound;
Nor hearken to a false report,
  By malice whisper'd round.

4
The Man who by this steady course,
  Hath happiness insured,
When earths, foundation shakes, shall stand,
  By Providence secured.

2

Thou, Lord, when I resign my Breath,
My Soul from Hell shall free;
Nor let thy holy One in Death
The least Corruption see.

3

Thou shalt the paths of Life display,
Which to thy presence lead;
Where pleasures dwell without allay,
And Joys that never fade.

Messiah   Ps 19.th C.M.   Handel

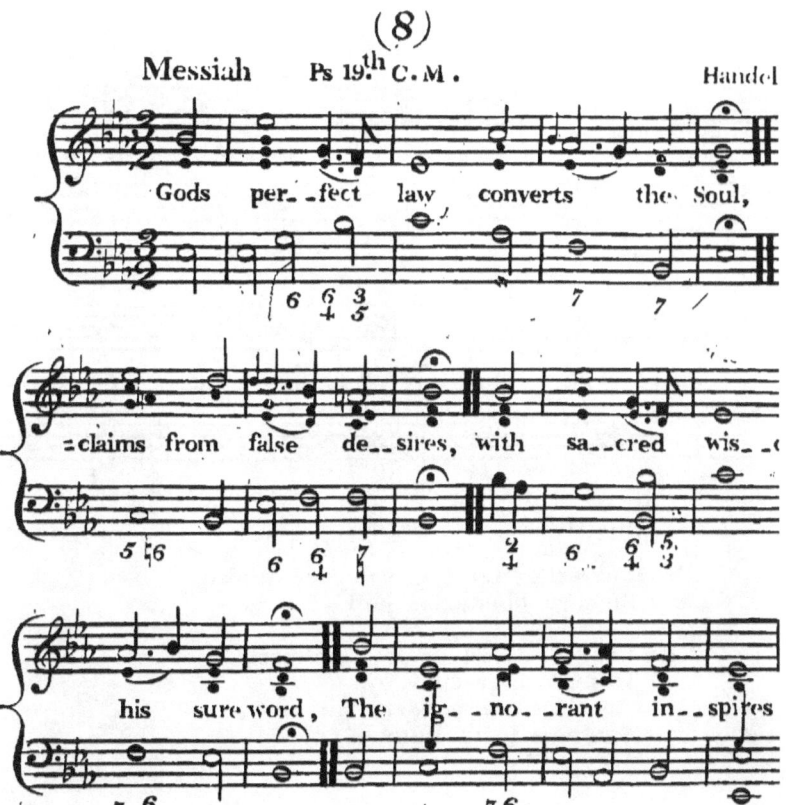

2
The statutes of the Lord are just,
   And bring sincere delight;
His pure commands in search of truth,
   Assist the feeblest sight.

3
His perfect worship here is fix'd,
   On sure foundations laid;
His equal Laws are in the scales,
   Of truth and justice weigh'd.

4
My trusty Counsellors they are,
   And friendly warnings give;
Divine rewards attend on those,
   Who by his precepts live.

"Ye worshipers of Jacobs God,
"All you of Israel's Line,
"O Praise the Lord and to your praise,
"Sincere obedience join.

"He ne'er disdain'd on low distress,
"To cast a gracious eye,
"Nor turn'd from poverty his face,
"But heard its humble cry.

3
I pass the gloomy vale of death,
 From fear and danger free;
For there his aiding rod and staff,
 Defend and comfort me.

4
Since God doth thus his wond'rous Love,
 Through all my life extend,
That life to him I will devote,
 And in his temple spend.

2
Those who on thee rely,
  Let no disgrace attend;
Be that the shameful lot of such,
  Who wilfully offend.

3
To me thy truth impart,
  And lead me in thy way;
For thou art He that brings me help:
  On thee I wait all day.

4
Thy mercies and thy Love,
  O Lord recall to mind;
And graciously continue still,
  As thou wert ever kind.

St. Matthews. Ps: 27 C.M.

3

Continue, Lord, to hear my Voice,
　Whene'er to Thee I cry;
In Mercy my Complaints receive,
　Nor my Requests deny.

4

When us to seek Thy glorious Face
　Thou kindly dost advise;
"Thy glorious Face I'll always seek,"
　My grateful Heart replies.

Let Earth, and all that dwell therein,
　Before Him trembling stand;
For, when he spake the Word, 'twas made,
　'Twas fix'd at His Command.

Whate'er the Mighty Lord decrees
　Shall stand for ever sure;
The settled Purpose of his Heart
　To Ages shall endure.

Abingdon. Ps: 34. C.M.

Thro' all the chang..ing scenes of trou..ble and in Joy. The prai..ses ..God shall still. My heart and Tongue er

2
Of this deliverance I will boast,
  Till all, that are distrest,
From my Example comfort take,
  And charm their griefs to rest.

3
O magnify the Lord with me,
  With me exalt his name:
When in distress to him I call'd,
  He to my rescue came.

4
Fear him, ye Saints, and you will then,
  Have nothing else to fear;
Make you his service your delight
  Your wants will be his Care.

Ps: 36 C.M.

Mr Westley.

O Lord thy mercy my sure hope, Above the Heavenly Orb, ascends; Thy sacred truth's unmeasured Scope Beyond the spreading Sky extends Beyond the spreading Sky extends.

2
Thy justice, like the Hills, remains;
    Unfathom'd Depths Thy Judgments are;
Thy Providence the World sustains;
    The whole Creation is Thy Care.

3
Since of Thy goodness all partake,
    With what Assurance should the just
Thy sheltering Wings their Refuge make,
    And Saints to Thy Protection trust:

4
Such Guests shall to Thy Courts be led
    To banquet on Thy Love's Repast;
And drink, as from a Fountains Head,

For God up--holds him with his

2

From my first youth, till age prevail'd,
I never saw the righteous fail'd,.
  Or want o'ertake his numerous race:
Because compassion fill'd his heart,
And he did chearfully impart,
  God made his Offspring's wealth increase.

3

Observe the perfect Man with Care,
And mark all such as upright are,
  Their roughest Days in peace shall end;
While on the latter end of those,
Who dare God's sacred will oppose,
  A common ruin shall attend.

Ps: 40 L.M.

2
I've learnt, that thou hast not desired
Off'rings and Sacrifice alone;
Nor Blood of guiltless Beasts required
For Man's Transgressions to atone.

3
I therefore come, —— come to fulfill
The Oracles Thy Books impart:
'Tis my Delight to do thy Will;
Thy Law is written in my Heart.

4
To Father, Son and Holy Ghost,
The God whom Earth and Heaven adore,
Be Glory, as it was of old,
Is now, and shall be evermore.

2
Awake my Glory: Harp and Lute,
  No longer let your Strings be mute:
And I, my tuneful Part to take,
  Will with the early Dawn awake.

3
Thy Praises, Lord, I will resound,
  To all the listening Nations round:
Thy Mercy highest Heaven transcends;
  Thy Truth beyond the Clouds extends!

4
Be Thou, O God, exalted high!
  And, as Thy Glory fills the Sky,
So let it be on Earth display'd,

2
That so thy wonderous way
  May thro' the world be known;
Whilst distant Lands their tribute pay,
  And Thy Salvation own.

3
Let differing Nations join
  To Celebrate thy fame;
Let all the World, O Lord combine,
  To praise thy glorious name.

4
O let them shout and sing
  With joy and pious mirth;
For thou the righteous Judge and King,
  Shalt govern all the earth!

2
Be thou my strong abiding place,
  To which I may resort;
Tis thy decree that keeps me safe;
  Thou art my rock and fort

3
Thy constant care did safely guard,
  My tender Infant days;
Thou took'st me from my Mother's womb,
  To sing thy constant praise.

4
Reject not then thy Servant Lord,
  When I with Age decay;
Forsake me not when worn with years;
  My vigour fades away.

(21)

Ps: 73 L. M.

Lord whom in heaven but thee alone Have I, I require? Throughout the spacious Earth there's I besides Thee can desire. Throughout the Earth there's none, That I besides Thee can de-

2
My trembling Flesh and aching Heart
  May often fail to succour me;
But God shall inward Strength impart,
  And my eternal Portion be.

3
For they, that far from thee remove,
  Shall into sudden Ruin fall;
If after other Gods they rove,
  Thy Vengeance shall destroy them all.

4
But as for me,'tis good and just
  That I should still to God repair;
In him I always put my Trust,
  And will his wond'rous Works declare.

Witton   Ps 77.th   C.M.

Safe lodg'd from human search on high, O God thy Counsels are! Who is so great a God as ours? Who can with him compare?

2
Long since a God of wonders thee
  Thy rescued People found:
Long since hast thou thy chosen seed
  With strong deliverance crown'd.

3
I'll call to mind thy works of old,
  The wonders of thy might;
On them my heart shall meditate
  My tongue shall them recite.

4
To Father, Son, And holy Ghost,
  The God whom we adore,
Be glory as it was, is now;
  And shall be evermore!

2
My longing Soul faints with desire,
  To view thy blest abode,
My panting heart and flesh cry out,
  For thee the living God!
3
Thrice happy they whose choice has thee,
  Their sure protection made;
Who long to tread the sacred ways,
  That to thy dwelling lead!
4
For in thy courts one single day,
  'Tis better to attend,
Than Lord, in any place besides,
  A thousand days to spend!

His tender Love and watchful care,
  Shall free thee from the fowler's snare,
And from the noisome Pestilence:
  He over thee his wings shall spread,
  And cover thy unguarded head;
His truth shall be thy strong defence.

4
To Father, Son, and Holy Ghost,
  The God, whom heaven's triumphant Host,
And suffering Saints on earth adore,
  Be glory as in ages past,
  As now it is, and so shall last,
When time itself shall be no more.

2
The Floods, O Lord, lift up their voice,
    And toss the troubled Waves on high;
But God above can still their Noise,
    And make the angry Sea comply.

3
Thy promise, Lord, is ever sure;
    And they, that in thy House would dwell,
That happy Station to secure,
    Must still in Holiness excell.

2
Into his presence let us haste,
  To thank him for his favors past;
To him address in joyful Songs,
  The praise that to his name belongs!

3
For God the Lord enthron'd in state,
  Is with unrival'd glory great;
A King superior far to all
  Whom Gods the heathens falsely call!

4
O let us to his courts repair,
  And bend with Adoration there;
Low on our knees devoutly all
  Before the Lord our maker fall!

2
Thou; Lord of all! art seated high,
 Above earth's potentates enthron'd!
Thou, Lord, unrival'd in the Sky,
 Supreme by all the Gods art own'd!

3
Ye, who to serve the Lord aspire,
 Abhor what's ill and truth esteem;
He'll keep his Servants, souls entire
 And them from wicked hands redeem.

4
Rejoice, ye righteous, in the Lord!
 Memorials of his holiness,
Deep in your faithful Breasts record,
 And with your thankful Tongues confess.

2
Convinced that He is God alone,
  From whom both we and all proceed,
We, whom He chuses for his own,
  The Flock that He vouchsafes to feed.

3
O enter then His Temple Gate,
  Thence to His Courts devoutly press
And still your grateful Hymns repeat,
  And still His Name with Praises bless.

4
For He's the Lord, supremely good
  His Mercy is for ever sure
His Truth, which always firmly stood,
  To endless Ages shall endure!

3

The Lord abounds with tender love
  And unexampled Acts of Grace;
His waken'd Wrath doth slowly move,
  His willing Mercy flies apace.

4

God will not always harshly chide,
  But with His Anger quickly part;
And loves His Punishments to guide
  More by His Love than our Desert.

With light as a robe
Thou hast thyself clad,
Whereby all the earth
Thy greatness may see!
The heav'ns in such sort
Thou also hast spread,
That they to a Curtain
Compared may be!

His chamber beams lie
In the clouds full sure,
Which as his Chariots,
Are made him to bear!
And there with much swiftness
His Course doth endure,
Upon the wings riding
Of winds in the Air!

4
He maketh his spirits
As heralds to go;
And lightnings to serve
We see also prest!
His will to accomplish
They run to and fro,
To save and consume things
As seemeth him best.

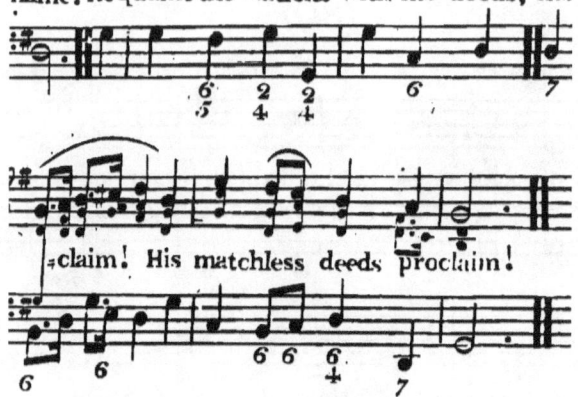

2
Sing to his praise! in lofty Hymns,
His wond'rous Works rehearse,
Make them the theme of your discourse,
And subject of your verse!

3
Rejoice in his Almighty name,
Alone to be adored;
And let their Hearts o'erflow with joy.
That humbly seek the Lord!

4
Seek ye the Lord! his saving strength,
Devoutly still implore,
And where he's ever present seek,
His Face for evermore!

2

Who can his mighty deeds express,
Not only vast—but numberless?
What mortal Eloquence can raise
His tribute of immortal Praise?

3

Happy are they, and only they,
Who from thy Judgments never stray;
Who know what's right,—not only so,
But always practise what they know.

4

Extend to me that Favour, Lord,
Thou to thy chosen dost afford;
When thou return'st to set them free,
Let thy Salvation visit me!

Meclenburgh   Ps 107th L.M.   Bach

2
No sooner his command is past,
But forth the dreadful tempest flies,
Which sweeps the Sea with rapid haste,
And makes the stormy billows rise!

3
Distress'd to God they make their pray'r!
Obedient to his sovereign will,
The storms that rage their rage forbear,
The boisterous Seas that roar'd are still.

4
O then that Men would thus with me,
The Lord for all his goodness praise,
And for the mighty works, which he,
Throughout the wondering world displays!

2
To all the list'ning Tribes, O Lord,
Thy wonders will I tell;
And to those Nations sing thy Praise,
That round about us dwell.

3
Because thy mercy's boundless Height
The highest Heaven transcends,
And far beyond th'aspiring Clouds
Thy faithful Truth extends.

4
Be thou, O God, exalted high
Above the starry Frame;
And let the World with one consent
Confess thy glorious Name.

St. Dunstans. Ps. 111th L.M.

Praise ye the Lord! our God to Praise My Soul her Powers shall raise; With private Friends, and in the throng of Saints, his praise shall be my Song! Of Saints his praise shall be

2
His Works, for Greatness tho' renown'd,
  His wond'rous Works with Ease are found,
By those, who seek for them aright,
  And in the pious Search delight.

3
His Works are all of matchless Fame
  And universal Glory claim;
His Truth, confirm'd thro' Ages past,
  Shall to eternal Ages last!

4
Who Wisdom's sacred Prize would win
  Must with the Fear of God begin;
Immortal Praise, and heavenly Skill
  Have they, who know and do his Will.

All Saints Ps 113th Ganthony

God thro' the world extends his sway,
The regions of eternal day,
But shadows of his glory are,
With him whose majesty excells,
Who made the heav'n in which he dwells,
Let no created power compare!

3
Tho' 'tis beneath his state to view,
In highest heaven what Angels do,
Yet he to earth vouchsafes his care,
He takes the needy from his Cell,
Advancing him in courts to dwell,
Companion to the greatest there!

Bedford   Ps 115th C.M.   W. Wheal M.B.

Lord not to us we claim no share, But to thy sa_cred name, give glo_ry for thy mercy's sake, And truths e_ter_nal fame.

2

Why should the Heathen cry, "Where's now,
"The God whom they adore,"
Convince them that in Heaven Thou art,
And uncontroll'd Thy Power.

3

Let all, who truly fear the Lord,
On Him they fear, rely;
Who them in danger can defend,
And all their Wants supply.

4

They, who in death and silence sleep,
To Him no Praise afford;
But we will bless for evermore,
Our ever living Lord.

2
Then open wide the Temple Gates,
 To which the Just repair,
That I may enter in, and praise,
 My great deliverer there!.

3
Within those Gates of God's Abode
 To which the Righteous press,
Since Thou hast heard and sett me safe
 Thy holy Name I'll bless.

4
Thou art my Lord, O God, and still
 I'll praise Thy holy Name!
Because Thou only art my God,
 I'll celebrate Thy Fame.

St. Andrews Ps 119th C.M. Phill: Hart.

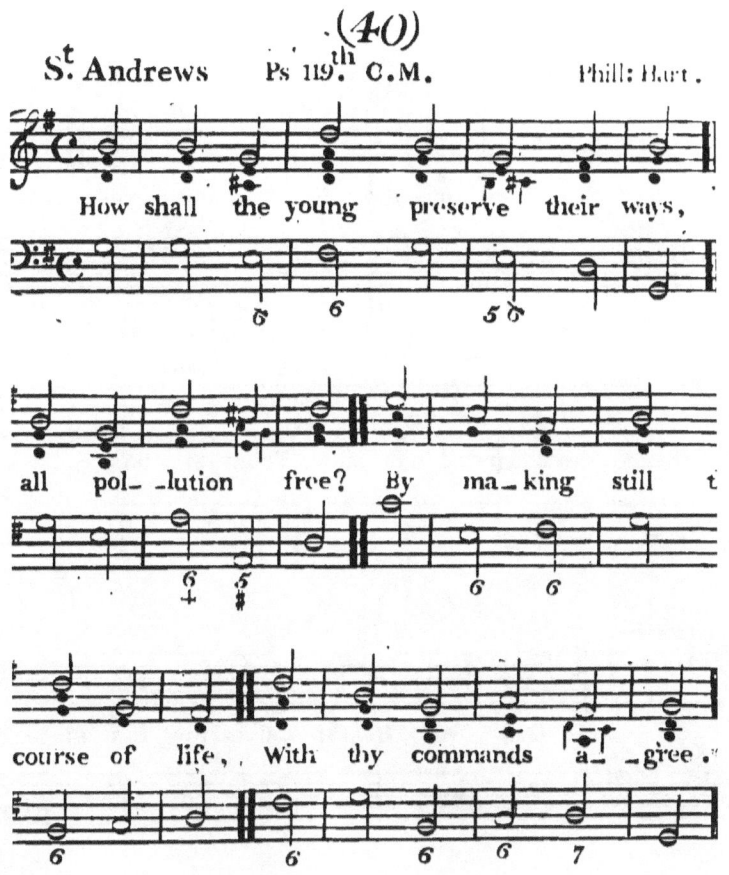

2
With hearty Zeal for Thee I seek,
To Thee for Succour pray;
O suffer not my careless Steps,
From Thy right Paths to stray.

3
Safe in my Heart, and closely hid
Thy Word, my Treasure, lies,
To succour me with timely Aid,
When sinful Thoughts arise.

4
Secured by that, my grateful Soul,
Shall ever bless Thy Name!
O teach me, then, by thy just Laws,
My future Life to frame!

2
Shelter'd beneath th' Almighty's Wings,
    Thou shalt securely rest;
Where neither Sun nor Moon shall thee,
    By Day or Night molest.

3
From common Accidents of Life,
    His Care shall guard thee still;
From the blind Strokes of Chance, and Foes,
    That lie in wait to kill.

4
At home, abroad, in peace, in war,
    Thy God shall thee defend;
Conduct thee thro' Life's Pilgrimage,
    Safe to thy Journey's End.

2
All those who walk in crooked Paths,
　The Lord shall soon destroy,
Cut off th'unjust, but crown the Saints,
　With lasting Peace and joy.

3
The wicked may afflict the just,
　But ne'er too long oppress,
Nor force him by despair to seek,
　Base means for his redress.

4
Be good O righteous God to those,
　Who righteous deeds affect,
The heart that Innocence retains,
　Let Innocence protect.

Mount Ephraim   Ps: 130th C.M.   Milgrove

From lowest depths of woe, To God I sent my cry; Lord hear my supplicating voice, And graciously reply.

2
My Soul with patience waits
 For thee the living Lord;
My hopes are on thy promise built,
 Thy never failing word.

3
Let Israel trust in God,
 No Bounds his mercy knows;
The plenteous source and Spring from whence
 Eternal Succour flows:

4
Whose friendly streams to us
 Supplies in want convey;
A healing Spring, A Spring to cleanse

2
Such Love is like the precious Oil
   Which pour'd on Aaron's head
Ran down his Beard and oe'r his Robes
   Its costly Moisture shed

3
'Tis like refreshing dew which does
   On Hermon's Top distill;
Or like the early drops that fall
   On Sion's fruitful Hill

4
For Sion is the chosen seat,
   Where the Almighty King
The promis'd blessing has ordain'd
   And life's eternal Spring.

St. James's Chapel Ps 135th C.M. Mr G.T. Smart

O Praise the Lord with one con-sent, And Mag-ni-fy his name, Let all the Ser-vants of the Lord, his wor-thy praise proclaim.

2
Praise him all ye that in his house,
Attend with constant care,
With those that to his utmost Courts,
With humble zeal repair!

3
For this our truest Int'rest is,
Glad Hymns of praise to sing,
And with loud Songs to bless his name,
A most delightful thing!

4
For God his own peculiar choice,
The Sons of Jacob makes,
And Israel's offspring for his own,
Most valued treasure takes.

2

To him, whose wond'rous power
All other Gods obey,
Whom earthly Kings adore,
This grateful homage pay!
For God does prove,
Our constant Friend,
His boundless love,
Shall never end!

3

By his Almighty hand,
Amazing works are wrought!
The Heav'ns by his command,
Were to perfection brought!
For God does prove,
Our constant Friend,
His boundless love,
Shall never end!

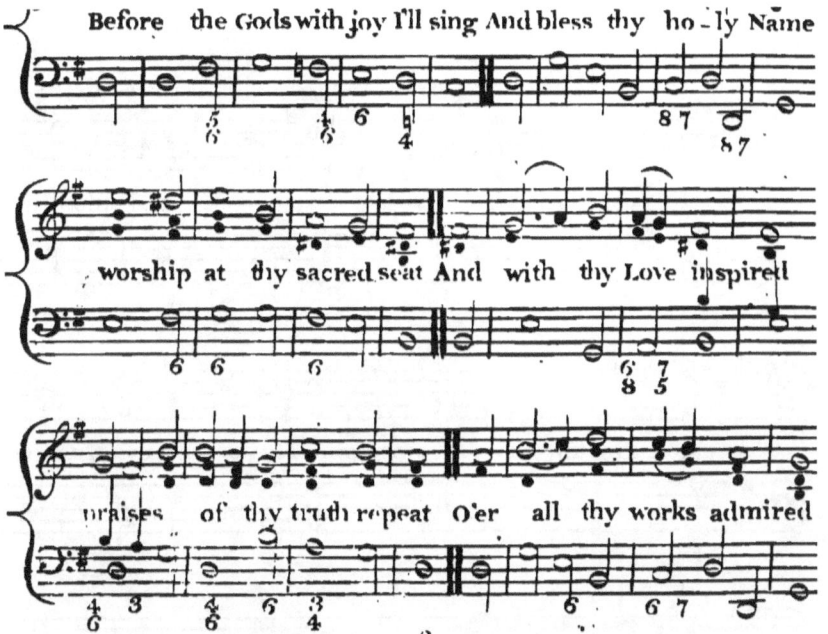

3
Thou graciously inclind'st thine Ear,
　　When I to thee did cry;
And when my Soul was press'd with fear,
　　Didst inward strength supply.

4
The Lord whose mercies ever last,
　　Shall fix my happy state;
And mindful of his favours past,
　　Shall his own works complete.

2

Thine eye my Bed and Path surveys,
My Public Haunts and private ways,
Thou know'st what e'er my lips would vent,
My yet unutter'd words Intent

3

Surrounded by thy power I stand,
On every side I find thy hand!
O skill, for human reach too high!
Too dazling bright for mortal eyes!

4

Let me acknowledge, O my God,
That, since this maze of Life I trod,
Thy thoughts of Love, to me surmount
The power of Numbers to recount!

Bedford Chapel Ps 145th C.M.

2
Thou Lord beyond compare art great,
And highly to be prais'd;
Thy Majesty, with boundless height,
Above our knowledge raised.

3
Renown'd for mighty Acts, thy fame
To future time extends,
From Age to Age thy glorious name
Successively descends.

4
Whilst I thy glory, and renown,
And wond'rous works express,
The world with me thy might shall own,
And thy great pow'r confess!

Cambridge   Ps 146th C.M.

The Lord who made both heav'n and earth, And all that they contain, Will never quit his steadfast truth, Nor make his promise vain, Nor make his promise vain, Nor make his promise vain.

2
The Poor, opprest from all their wrongs
  Are eased by his decree;
He gives the hungry needful food,
  And sets the Pris'ners free.

3
By him the blind receive their sight,
  The weak and faln He rears,
With kind regard and tender love
  He for the righteous cares.

4
The God, that doth in Sion dwell,
  Is our eternal King;
From Age to Age his reign endures;
  Let all his praises sing!

2
He kindly heals the broken hearts
And all the wounds doth close,
He tells the Number of the Stars;
Their sev'ral Names he knows:

3
Great is the Lord, and great his pow'r,
His wisdom has no bound!
The meek he raises, and throws down,
The wicked to the ground!

4
The Lord to him, that fears his name,
His tender Love extends,
To him, that on his boundless grace
With stedfast hope depends.

2
Thou Moon that rul'st the Night,
And Sun that guid'st the Day,
Ye glittering stars of light,
To him your homage pay!
His praise declare,
Ye heavens above,
And Clouds that move
In liquid Air!

3
Let them Adore the Lord,
And praise his holy name,
By whose Almighty word
They all from nothing came:
And all shall last
From changes free!
His firm decree
Stands ever fast!

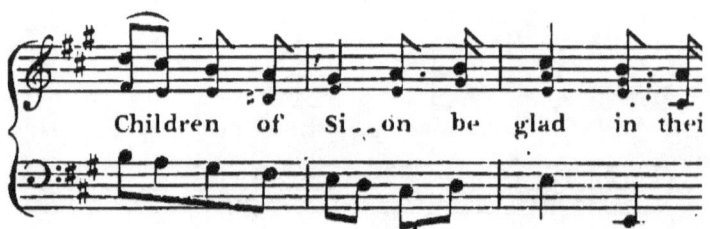

Children of Si-on be glad in thei[r]

2

Let them his great Name
 Extoll in the dance;
With Timbrel and Harp
 His praises express,
Who always takes pleasure
 His Saints to advance,
And with his Salvation
 The humble to bless!

3

By Angels in Heaven
 Of every Degree,
And Saints upon Earth
 All praise be address'd
To God in three Persons,
 One God ever blest;
As it has been, now is,
 And always shall be!

2
Praise Him on Earth for all the Acts
   Which He in our Behalf hath done!
His Kindness this Return exacts,
   With which our Praise should equal run!

3
Let all, that vital Breath enjoy,
   The Breath He does to them afford
In just Returns of Praise employ!
   Let every Creature praise the Lord!

4
To Father, Son, and Holy Ghost,
   The God whom Earth and Heaven adore
Be Glory, as it was of old,
   Is now, and shall be evermore!

MORNING HYMN 1 L.M. Mr G.T. Smart

Awake my Soul and with the Sun, Thy daily stage of duty run! Shake off dull sloth and early rise to pay thy morning sacrifice.

2
Lord I my vows to thee renew,
Scatter my Sins as Morning dew!
Guard my first spring of thought and will,
And with thyself my Spirit fill.

3
Direct, controul, suggest, this day,
All I design, or do or say;
That all my pow'rs, with all their might,
May in thy glory Lord unite!

4
Glory to God who safe hath kept,
Who hath refresh'd me while I slept!
O, may I, when from death I wake,
Thro' him an endless Life partake!

5
Praise God from whom all blessings flow,
Praise him, all Creatures here below!
Praise him above, Angelic Host,
Praise Father, Son, and Holy Ghost!

(This Hymn may had printed singly.)

2
The Evil, I this day have done,
Forgive, O Lord thro' Christ thy Son!
That with the world, myself, and thee,
I ere I sleep, at peace may be!

3
Teach me to live, that I may dread,
The Grave as little as my bed!
Teach me to die, that so I may,
With joy behold the judgement day!

4
O may my Soul on Thee repose!
Thou with soft sleep my eyelids close!
Sleep, that may me more active make,
To serve my God when I awake!

5
Praise God, from whom all blessings flow,
Praise him, all Creatures here below!
Praise him above, Angelic Host.
Praise Father, Son, and holy Ghost.

3
Seasons renew'd, and Years and days,
Demand successive Songs of praise;
Still be the grateful homage paid,
With opening light, and evening shade!

4
O may we, with harmonious tongue,
In realms above pursue the Song!
There in those brighter Courts adore,
Where days and Years revolve no more!

3
Oh what is Man that in thy mind,
His humble lot should have a share?
Or what his Sons that thus they find,
Their wants the object of thy care?

4
All that a grateful heart can give,
Is poor to what thy love demands!
Yet Lord accept us while we strive,
T'obey in fear thy blest commands!

3

The heavenly heritage is theirs,
　Their Portion and their home,
He feeds them now, and makes them heirs,
　Of blessings long to come.

4

Wait on the Lord ye Sons of Men,
　Nor fear when Tyrants frown,
Ye shall confess their Pride was vain,
　When justice casts them down!

The Christian Hope Hymn 6 Lent C.M.

When thou, O Lord, shall stand disclos'd, In Majesty severe, And sit in judgement on my Soul, Oh, how shall I appear!

2
But thou hast told the troubled mind,
   Who does her Sins lament,
The timely tribute of her tears
   Shall endless woe prevent!

3
Then see the Sorrows of my heart,
   Ere yet it be too late!
And hear my Saviour's dying groans
   To give those sorrows weight!

4
For never shall my Soul despair
   Her pardon to procure:
Who knows thine only Son has died
   To make that Pardon sure!

Burford. Hymn 7 Good Friday. C.M.

From whence those dire portents around, that
Earth and heav'n amaze? wherefore do Earthquake
cleave the ground? Why hides the Sun his rays?

2
See streaming from the fatal tree,
His all atoning Blood!
Is this the Saviour? — yes, 'tis he!
My Saviour and my God!

3
Wisdom and grace united wrought
The wonders of that day!
No mortal tongue, nor mortal thought,
Can equal thanks repay!

4
Let Sin no more my Soul enslave;
Break, Lord, the tyrants chain
Save me, thou Lamb, sent down to save,
Nor bleed for me in vain!

2
Hymns of Praises let us sing, Hallelujah!
Unto Christ our heavenly King, Hallelujah!
Who endured the Cross and grave, Hallelujah!
Sinners to redeem and save! Hallelujah!

3
But the Pains which he endur'd, Hallelujah!
Our Salvation have procur'd! Hallelujah!
Now he reigns above the Sky, Hallelujah!
Where the Angels ever cry. Hallelujah!

Oxford Chapel Hymn 9 Ascension L.M. Mr Parrin

Our Lord is risen from the Dead, The Saviour is gone up on high; The powers of hell are captive led, Drag'd to the Portals of the Sky! There his Triumphal Chariot waits, And Angels chaunt the solemn lay, Lift up your heads Lift up your heads lift up your heads ye heav'nly Gates! ye everlasting doors give way!

2d Verse

Loose all your bars of massive light, | Who is the King of glory?——Who
And wide unfold th'etherial Scene! | The Lord that all his foes o'ercam
He claims these mansions as his right; | The World Sin death & hell o'erthr
Receive the King of glory in! | And Jesus is the conquerors name

2
In every clime in every tongue,
Be Gods eternal praises sung!
Thro' all the list'ning earth be taught
The Acts our great redeemer wrought!
Thro' all the list'ning earth be taught
The Acts our great redeemer wrought!

3
Unfailing comfort heavenly guide,
Over thy favorite Church preside!
Still may Mankind thy blessings prove
Spirit of mercy truth and love!
Still may Mankind thy blessings prove
Spirit of mercy, truth, and love!

2
Therefore, their great creator, thee
　The Nations shall adore;
Their long misguided prayers and praise
　To thy blest name restore!

3
All shall confess thee great and great
　The wonders thou hast done!
Confess Thee God the God supreme,
　Confess Thee God alone.

4
To Father, Son, and holy Ghost,
　The God whom we adore,
Be glory as it was, is now,
　And shall be evermore!

(68)

Ormskirk Hymn 12 May 29th P.L.M. Mr. Parrin

Tho' wicked Men grow rich or great, Yet let not their suc-cessful state, Thy anger or thy envy raise, For they cut down like tender grass, Or like young flow'rs a way shall pass, Whose blooming beauty soon decays.

2
Depend on God, and him obey;
So thou within the Land shalt stay,
Secure from danger and from want;
Make his commands thy chief delight,
And he thy duty to requite;
hall all thy earnest wishes grant.

3
In all thy ways trust thou the Lord,
And he will needful help afford,
To perfect every just design;
He'll make like light serene and clear,
Thy clouded Innocence appear,
And as the mid day Sun to Shine.

Hymn 13* The Kings Accession

Mr. Parrin

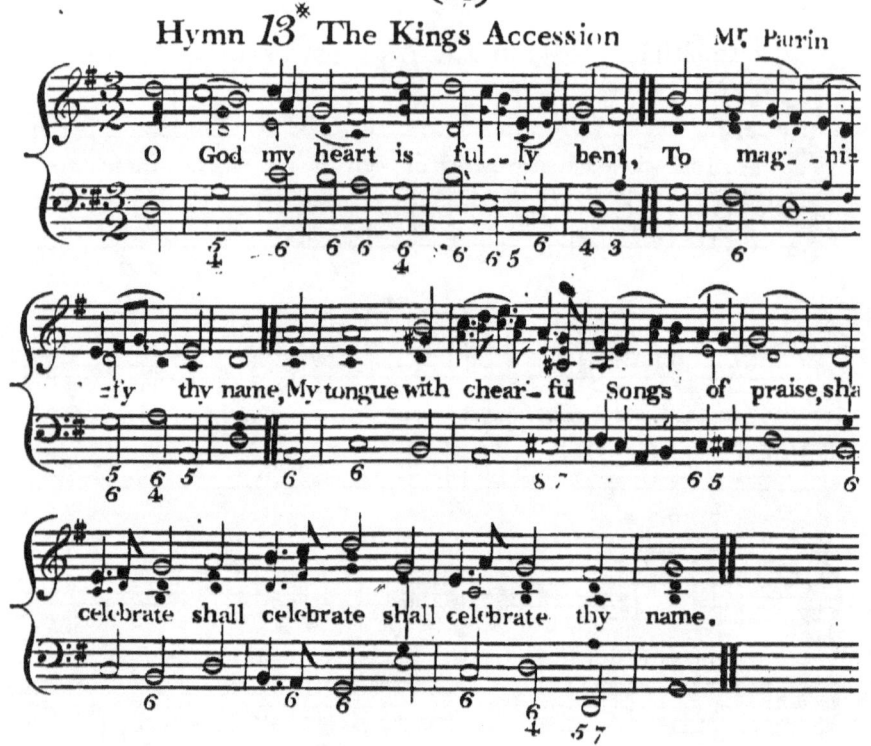

O God my heart is ful—ly bent, To mag—ni—fy thy name, My tongue with chear—ful Songs of praise, sha celebrate shall celebrate shall celebrate thy name.

2

To all the list'ning tribes, O Lord,
   Thy wonders I will tell;
And to those Nations sing thy praise,
   That round about us dwell.

3

The Lord from heaven beholds the just,
   With favourable eyes;
And when distress'd his gracious ear,
   Is open to their cries.

4

The Lord preserves the Souls of those,
   Who on his truth depend,
To them and their posterity,

Hymn 14 November 5th C.M. Mr Lord

2
Their wrath had swallow'd us alive,
And raged without controul,
Their Hate and pride's united floods,
Had quite o'erwhelm'd our Soul.

3
But prais'd be our Eternal Lord,
Who rescued us that day,
Nor to their savage hands gave up,
Our threaten'd Lives a prey.

4
Secure in his Almighty name,
Our Confidence remains,
Who as he made both heaven and earth,
Of both sole Monarch reigns.

Baltimore Hymn 15 Advent C.M. Dr. Arne

Let Israel catch the joyful sound
Judahs daughters hear Tell all th'expect-
world around Messiahs Kingdoms near.

2
The weary Nations shall have rest,
Oppression's reign shall cease;
The teeming Earth henceforth be blest,
With Innocence and peace !

3
The sightless Eye shall now behold;
The Lame exulting spring;
Th'obstructed Ear its maze unfold,
And hear the dumb Man sing !

4
To Zion shall the ransom'd fly,
In Hymns their God adore;
The tear be wip'd from ev'ry eye,
And Sorrow be no more !

2

Good Will to Sinfull Man is shewn,
   And Peace on Earth is given!
For lo! th'incarnate Saviour comes
   With Messages from Heaven!

3

Glory to God, with humble heart,
   Let favour'd Man repay!
His Glory let our Lips proclaim,
   And let our Lives display!

4

Then shall we reach those blissful Realms
   Where Christ exalted reigns,
And learn of the celestial Choir
   Their own immortal Strains!

Hymn 17 Sacrament C.M. Mr Lord

In Innocence I wash my hands, And so encompass round, Thine Altar with th' sacred bands, Whose tongues thy praises sound

2
How oft, inspired with warmth divine,
 Thy threshold have I trod!
How lov'd the Courts, whose walls enshrine,
 The Glory of my God!

3
Pour then O Pour while thus I tread,
 The paths by thee prepar'd,
Thy beams of mercy on my head,
 And round me plant thy guard!

4
Hear me O God in Mercy hear,
 While I my guilt deplore;
Pity my anguish calm my fear,
 And let me sin no more!

2
O look for ever kindly down,
 On those that help the poor!
Oh let success their labours crown,
 And plenty heap their store!
Oh may that Mite which we've possest,
Diffuse a blessing o'er the rest!

3
And when before thy Judgement seat,
 With trembling hope we go,
Reward or Punishment to meet,
 For what we've done below,
Our shouting voices shall declare,
Their tender love to us while here!

2
The Lord his Life, with blessings crown'd,
  In safety shall prolong;
And dissappoint the will of those
  Who seek to do him wrong!

3
If he in languishing estate
  Oppress'd with sickness lie,
The Lord shall easy make his Bed,
  And inward strength supply.

4
Thy care, O Lord, secures his Life
  From danger and disgrace;
And thou vouchsaf'st to set him still
  Before thy glorious Face!.

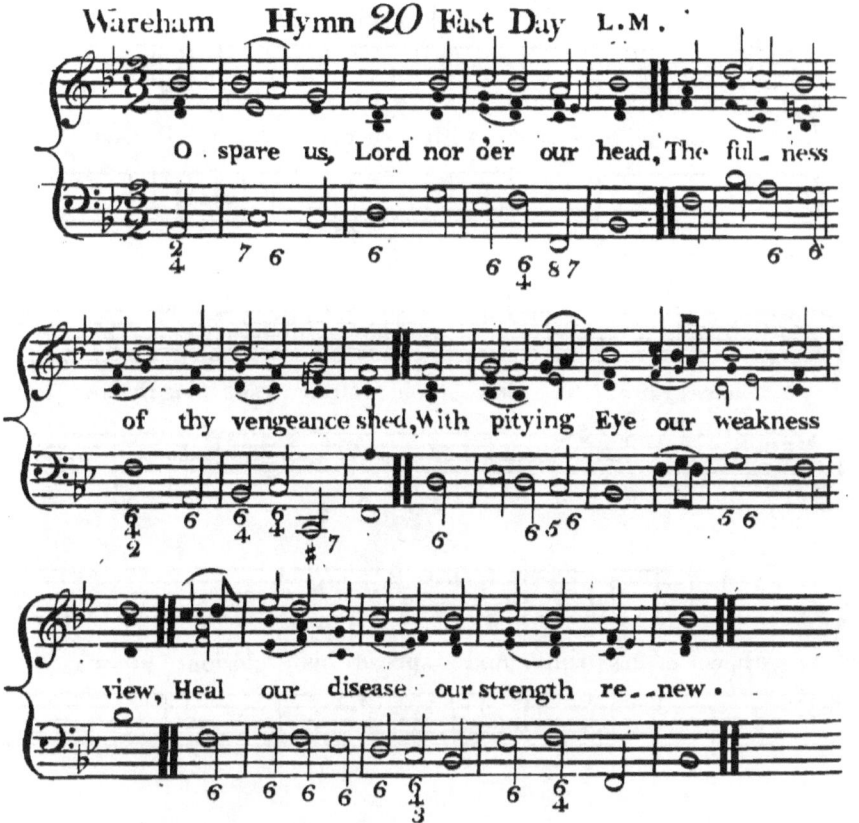

And O! if yet our Sins demand,
The wise corrections of thy hand,
Yet give our Pains their bounds to know,
And fix a Period to our woe!

To thee, great God, our hearts we bend,
To thee our ceaseless pray'rs ascend!
Return, O Lord! return, and save
Thy Servants from the threat'ning Grave!

O spare us, Lord! awhile O spare,
And Nature's ruin'd strength repair!
Our Trust in thee we still maintain

Hymn 21 Thanksgiving Day C.M. Mr Parrin

Let all the Lands, with shouts of joy, To God their voices raise! To God their voices raise, Sing Hymns in honor of his name, And spread his glorious praise.

2
And let them say How dreadful Lord,
  In all thy works art thou!
To thy great power thy stubborn foes,
  Shall all be forc'd to bow!

3
Thro' all the earth the Nations round,
  Shall Thee their God confess,
And in glad notes their awful dread,
  Of thy great name express!

4
O! come, behold the works of God,
  And then with me you'll own,
That he to all the Sons of Men,
  Has wond'rous judgement shewn!

Hymn 22 Funeral P. M. Adapted from Mr Batishills Chaunt.

Re—demption draweth nigh! My joy—ful lips shall sing, Where is thy boasted vict'ry Grave, O Death where is thy sting.

2
Hear what a voice proclaims,
  To all the pious Dead!
"Sweet the remembrance of their names,
  "Their Grave a resting Bed!

3
"In Christ, their Lord, they die,
  "Remov'd from Sin and care;
"From suff'ring and from pain releas'd,
  "And freed from ev'ry snare!

4
"Far from this world of Toil,
  "They wait their Judge and Lord,
"The Labours of a well spent Life,
  "He'll crown with just reward!

www.ingramcontent.com/pod-product-compliance
Lightning Source LLC
Chambersburg PA
CBHW030411170426
43202CB00010B/1564